Charles James

First Published in Great Britain in 1997
by Thames and Hudson Ltd. London

Copyright © 1997 Éditions Assouline, Paris

British Library Cataloguing-in-Publication Data

A catalogue record for this book is available from
the British Library
ISBN 0-500-01783-2

Printed and bound in Italy

Charles James

Text by Richard Martin

Thames and Hudson

a 1992 suite of photographs by Bruce Weber shows two muscle boys, bare to the waist, who stroke, caress and make love to a Stockman dress form inhabiting a Charles James ballgown. In one image, a bicep-bulging arm grasps the bust with ardent, adolescent lust while the other young man, eyes closed, swoons at the drapery. Here are two men enslaved to one Charles James dress, an idol of female beauty. James would have loved this photograph, which unleashes the ever-present sexuality of the dress and accompanies it with unabashed delight and eroticism. What James invested in the dress, Weber releases into a contemporary image. A chin touches tulle in orgasmic bliss; the boys' hands encircle the waist as if ready to dance with the dress; one boy rapturously kisses the shoulder of the dress form.

Decades older than its passionate admirers, the James dress stands as sensual sign and siren of utmost femininity. James consistently sought to establish a setting for the voluptuous female body, most often with a cinched, highly constricted waist, a firmly supported and even enhanced bust, and a luxury of materials in a broad skirt of Winterhalter crinoline-era dimensions. James gave edifice to lust and icon to the feminine. Even his French contemporary Christian Dior, who fixed on a similar silhouette in the 1940s and 1950s, achieved no image more concupiscent than James's dresses.

t he achievement of Charles James was to impart lust to the dress. Anyone who looks at a Charles James dress realizes that there is archetypal eroticism within and without. Yet, at the same time, the James garment is such a built environment, constructed on principles of abstraction but substantiated by ample materials, that the woman wearing it becomes curiously self-sufficient as well. Thus, a famous Cecil Beaton photograph of women in a ballroom is both a sign of the feminine and an indication of women's independent power, evoking Winterhalter's painting of the court of Empress Eugénie. Elsewhere, in the 'Sylphide' evening dress (1937), James had employed a corselette based on an 1860s example to cinch an organza and taffeta dress in the manner of the Second Empire. James was able to accept the lucrative commission to design dresses for the advertising of Modess sanitary napkins because his dresses suggested the tradition of the most powerful, elegant and delicate women in the world. James offered both dignity and desire in the same grand dress. In the 1940s and 1950s, needing to seek out a long-ago past sullied and interrupted by Holocaust and war, women strove to be these magnificent, sculptural creations that James constructed. Daring to return to nineteenth-century restraints and structure, James was able to offer an ideal, and flattering, shape to which every woman could conform, using the accommodations of built-in corsets and built-out flair and fullness. James's magic was to combine a science of design with an erotic of fashion. He knew bombast (literally, the paddings within a dress) and he recognized in it the sexy bombshell silhouettes of the 1940s and 1950s.

today, James is a fashion designer whose major works hang or stand in museum collections. His garments have achieved record prices at auction in 1976 and 1995; both acquisitions for museums. Yet, as the photographer Bill Cunningham noted (*The Soho Weekly News*, 28 September 1978) in an obituary of James, the designer believed in the dress as a sublime couture creation, dependent on the 'dialogue between the client and dressmaker', which, said James, 'no fashion world could exist without'.

Thus, according to James's own edict, we possess today only the dry bones of the designer's vital creation. James's acknowledgment of dialogue originates, too, in his first career as a milliner, in which he was inexorably involved with the face and mask of his client. Later, though he would display loyalty to some of his faithful clients, he was chiefly the creator of his own vision of woman as muse, an image which differentiated little from one client to another.

but James was also an egomaniacal misanthrope, capable of cutting the cords that bound him to other human beings, whether in business, society or personal life. He was the inspiring force for Halston, whom he reportedly introduced to Lily Daché, and yet he ended their friendship acrimoniously. He offended some of his most loyal clients, who longed for the designer's dresses and paid dearly for them, not only in money but in tolerating insults and abuse. The dialogue that James claimed fashion needed was for him more often a monologue of his own creative frenzy, stilling all other voices. He could be alternately charming and infuriating, turning ingratiation off and on with alacrity and self-indulgent delight. His patrons became either advocates or adversaries, the latter frustrated by false billings and delayed deliveries, the former as generous as Millicent Rogers, who not only bought James's dresses for herself, but for the Brooklyn Museum as well. James's admirers were ardent. In *Town & Country* (October

1949), American fashion writer Lois Long wrote: 'Had his talent led him towards architecture in stone instead of in cloth, the American flag would flap wildly as propagandists beat drums in praise of him. He is a prophet who enjoys full honors in Europe.'

born in 1906, James was a fashion independent and polymath in the manner of other beguiling mavericks such as Elizabeth Hawes and Cecil Beaton. He celebrated the world and purposefully sought out beauty, but he could also be cynical, caustic and malicious. Hawes exorcised her fashion demons in elegant and witty writing; Beaton's brittle address to society was so prolix that his slurs, even the famous ones, went largely forgiven; but James was mean and aggressive, even to those who tried to befriend him and his work. As Cunningham reports, 'James was more appreciated in the art world than the fashion world.' Of course, James was more intimate with the fashion world. He despised many of the business practices of fashion as commerce; he was admired, if less well-known, in the art world, where such patrons as Millicent Rogers, Austine Hearst, Dominique de Menil and Mrs Fritz Bultmann acted as graceful intermediaries and Antonio, the illustrator, served for a long time as most eloquent delineator. Had James actually been involved in the art world, it is likely that he would have worn out his welcome there as well. But those in the fashion world whose primary acquaintance was with the clothing rather than the designer found themselves able to give high praise to his work, as Christian Dior did, calling his designs 'poetry'.

for all the controversy surrounding James's volatile life, there was a consistent idealism in his work. He referred to nature as his source, but he actually created a scenic, picturesque effect. In the late 1940s and 1950s, many of his designs were named after living things, including the 'Petal', 'Swan', 'Tulip', 'Butterfly', 'Four-Leaf Clover' and 'Tree' dresses. From this it might seem as though James were an indefatigable naturalist, but a study of his drawings for these and similar gowns indicates otherwise. James is true to nature only in essence, in the manner of the sculptor Constantin Brancusi or the painter–sculptor Jean Arp. James seeks to absorb the essential from nature, not the complications of the real world. He seeks quintessential and reductive form, perceiving giant arcs in clovers or trees and grand crescents and semicircles in flowers as applicable to the human body. To be sure, there is an organic certainty in James's referencing of the natural forms, but his ambition is to make these forms abstract. James's arresting drawings – often on crude, lined notepapers – conceive of overriding shapes and grand gestures. If they look like sketches for Brancusi, it is because they are of a similar ethos.

Yet James did not execute his dresses wholly in the abstract spirit of his inspired drawings. He was required to build the dress within, as a dressmaker, to the silhouette so deftly realized in drawing. Hip poufs, winged side panels and constructed bodices were some of the devices that had to be employed in order for him to arrive at the spirally constructed and concentric forms that he cherished. The lyric, uncomplicated drawings could only be realized with the aid of a lot of stuff and stuffing. It is in this contradiction between abstract, gestural design and ponderous construction that James experiences his major difficulty. Another great dressmaker recognized the effort involved; Balenciaga praised him, saying, 'Charles James is not only the most eminent American couturier, but also the best, and the only one in the world who has raised haute couture from an applied art form to a pure art form.' Balenciaga himself was a master of form that could both cling to the body and stand on its own away from the body by virtue of the strength of the fabric or of the inner structure. He admired James's similar attainment, though perhaps partly in order to return attention to his own gift.

●

It was not only the design of his garments that James imagined but also their grandeur. A James dress is described in *Harper's Bazaar* (October 1946): 'Once again, the grand toilette . . . the costume of the moment, dressmaking in the superlative degree. Here, cobalt faille, festooned from hip to hip, the bodice folded to a point and held by a thin strap.' The magazine recognized that James, even before the House of Dior was founded, was contemplating a renewed magnificence, but one that was founded in modern principles of design. Austine Hearst testified to the experience of wearing a James gown: 'I will always remember the *magic* of wearing one of Charles James's ravishing, romantic ball-gowns, remember being transformed by him like Cinderella into a radiant princess.' His graphic silhouettes were perfect for the grand entry into a ballroom or for the shape-defining photograph. James was prodigiously well served by fashion photographers of the epoch, including Louise Dahl-Wolfe, Lillian Bassman, Cecil Beaton, Horst and Richard Avedon, who realized that his great concoctions of shape were essays in form. A strategically placed mirror, a bit of drapery or even a sublimely barren set would only enhance the inherent configuration of the garment or its photographic expression.

A famous Cecil Beaton photograph of 1948 poses together nine women in James ballgowns, the dresses' icy and pastel surfaces and deep troughs of material simulating the glacial eighteenth-century architecture of the room. The Beaton photograph shows off both James's consistency and his variations, each dress being different, but all aiming toward a similar ideal. Asymmetrical necklines, strapless dresses, bodies of different colours from skirts, and deep décolletages tell the stories of a single ideal of convivial feminine beauty wrapped in an extravagance of fabric. Beaton realized the sense of musical variation in James's many efforts to compose the ideal dress. He very likely recognized the connection to Winterhalter; these bare shoulders and spacious forms of the 1940s were harking back nearly a century. Of course, James was thinking of strapless dresses in a modern, mid-century manner, but the gestures and the harmony of these soignée women is distinctly reminiscent of their Second Empire predecessors. Thus, later American designer Marc Jacobs said acutely of James, 'He understood human nature, how people want to adorn themselves and be spectacular.' James appreciated the spectacular.

L ike Dior, James delighted in creating a hard carapace by which the dress could conform to his supposed engineering. He pretended to give serious thought to the structuring elements of the dress, but a study of most of the dresses shows that he simply applied more and more layers until he achieved the needed density and shape. There are exceptions: his soft padded coat of 1937 and other helical coats and wraps were more or less pure form. But most of the ballgowns had to be fabricated like something out of an ironworks. Lest the result seem too massive, James finished even the most armoured dress with softly affixed layers of pliant materials that wrapped around the rigid structure. If in receiving an elegant gift box, we are more aware of the fancy ribbon than of the box itself, we know what it is to see a James dress. The soft, attached drapery is so seductive as a surface that we are almost unaware of the rigid shell inside. James was decidedly superficial; the dress could very nearly stand up on its own, so filled was it with materials, but the picturesque effect was that of a dream walking. Some James dresses are reportedly nearly fifty pounds in weight, but their engineering balance made them wearable. Even more than engineering, what James achieved was the suspension of disbelief. The visible impression of these dresses was gossamer and mellifluous; many women were willing to carry a nineteenth-century weight in order to achieve the graceful James shape with its weightless demeanour. Compared with the capricious treatment James's legendary clients had already endured from their designer, the mere hauling around of a heavy dress was a minor burden. What such women attained was a certainty that in these dresses they were suave and exquisite. Patrick O'Higgins has compared them to ships in full sail.

In commenting on James in *Interview* (July 1992), Bill Cunningham recognized that 'he presented women with a shape that was not their own. You went in to Charles James deformed, and you came out a *Venus de Milo*. He was the equivalent of someone from the Renaissance who made ceremonial armors.' James's transfiguration of the client was possible because he had an unflinching ideal of the perfect woman in his mind and in his work. Loyal clients felt beautiful in James's Pygmalion-like reformation of the real body into a perfect Galatea. His purpose in imposing clothing was to correct nature and to allow a real woman with body faults to feel and act as if she were flawless. There are always design secrets in James's garments, some of which are concealed in mass, but many of which come from fundamental principles of design. The James waist is invariably cut on the curve, enjoying the swooping uncertainty of the natural waist and the designed waist. Of course, other designers, such as Balenciaga and Geoffrey Beene, work in a like manner, but James realized the woman's own idiosyncratic concentric form in spiralling around the waist. James boasted that he bypassed bust darts, but he accomplished this primarily by having many pattern pieces converge at the bust to create a shaping rather like that of a well-made brassiere. Yet such inventions were largely obscured within the dress's outer face, veiled as it was in softly affixed drapery.

although James is best known for his extravagant evening dresses, one of his greatest achievements was his coats and capes, many inspired by North African capes and caftans. In such instances, his usual construction is often restrained in favour of capes as loose as a caftan or wraps with dolman sleeves. In a 1949 drawing for a Chesterfield coat, James expertly inserts pockets in the seams and demonstrates the arc of seam lines that rises to its uppermost at centre front. A box pleat at the back allows for a fluidity of movement that is not apparent from the front. In dresses, James would often hide a pleat within the construction to allow for some flex, but here he makes the softness apparent, if only at the back. James's 1930s coats are, like those of many of his contemporaries, including Grès and Lanvin, minimally constructed to sweep with a ribbony openness. His late 1930s 'Ribbon' evening cape is a petal shape with ribbons and wings. Many stand-up collars reflect the circular gyration of the coat's pattern pieces, continuing Grès' tailoring with dressmaker-like pliant pieces forced into three-dimensionality. The cocoon was again and again a model for James's coats. The 'Gothic' coat, which he repeated often in the 1950s, was an A-line cone with a simulation of an Empire waist in satin. In fact, the coats continue the investigation that James initiated in his famous 'Taxi' dress of around 1929–30, a spiral wrapped dress said to be so easy to wear that it can be put on in the back seat of a taxi. Bias-cut cloth wraps the body one and a half times, closing first with clasps and in later versions with a zipper. This dress, in the manner of Vionnet, Valentina and Grès, was largely abandoned by James and its ideas were pursued in the coats until, in the 1960s and 1970s, James returned to these simple studies in bias. The James–Halston collaboration at this time ended in bitter dispute over such designs, but it seems certain that James was at least an interme-diary and an inspiring force who awakened Halston to the bias drape and body consciousness of the 1930s.

n or did James entirely abandon his 1930s roots. His 1944 dinner sheath, remaking an earlier model, photographed in *Vogue* (1 October 1944) modelled by Marlene Dietrich, continues the tradition of 1930s dresses into the war years. This daring dress is slit to the skin asymmetrically from shoulder to hip, and tied across with five satin bows of the same fabric as the dress. It is a tour-de-force combination of sportswear wrapping and body-clinging eveningwear. *Vogue* acknowledged that it was a 'characteristic Charles James original'. His 'Sirène' evening dress of around 1938, which he repeated in 1955–56, renewed the suppleness of both his own 1930s dresses and those of other designers. Here, small arcs of manipulated cloth fall into slinky rhythms of movement as the wearer moves, the effect being almost like that of an animal's skin. One can understand how inspiring such a dress would be to the designers of the 1970s; illustrator Antonio's rendering of it made it a paradigm for contemporary dress in both that decade and the 1980s. Shirring and bias cut had an appeal in the 1970s. For Antonio, this dress was a Surrealist transfiguration as well as a seductive siren. In silhouette, it became a signal for the 1970s, though few of the soft dresses of those years were constructed in the manner of the James. He had imparted structure at centre front by causing the 'spine' (the funnel-shaped front panel of the dress) to splay outward to the soft radiating arcs in cascade. But even here he had been unwilling to yield entirely to the fluid principles of the 1930s; he alone insisted on keeping a dense, weighty core from which lines flowed. A 1992 soft-focus photograph by Paolo Roversi of the 'Sirène' makes the dress an ideal in silhouette on a dress form, but also poses an ephebic male nude with the lower portion of the dress which serves as both mother-love and erotic love for the young man whose nude back and buttocks confirm and continue the soft oval of the dress's shape.

a t the opposite extreme in historical reference and in design is James's 'Balloon' dress of *circa* 1955, a grand ballgown with Empire waist leading toward a prominent curved polonaise deeply descending in the front, but rising up toward the back. Here, James demonstrates his virtuoso sense of history along with his virtuoso talent for dressmaking. The dress threatens to lose form altogether in billowing scale, but James swoops the polonaise down to recover the shape of what appears to be an underskirt below. The 'Lampshade' evening gown (1953) is exemplary of the interest James showed from 1948 through the 1950s in kicking out to a wide circumference only at the knee, keeping the hips tightly wrapped. In 'Lampshade', a reminder of Paul Poiret's designs in the 1910s, James devised a figure-eight knee-line flounce, enhancing the silhouette of a strapless fitted bodice, padded hips with clinging drapery, and the wide lengthening below the knee. The 'Tulip' ballgown (1949) had proposed a similar silhouette with wide flounce. Initially, James achieved the volume of the flounce through boning, but later versions of the 1950s, as construction lightened in all fashion, eliminated the boning as too severe and traditional. It may also have been restrictive to walking and certainly added to the weight of the dress. As in other examples, clients did not complain about the heavy weights, but the dresses must have been cumbersome and uncomfortable to wear.

In between James's bouffant ballgowns and his decorous shapes inspired by the 1930s are the evening gowns drawn from nature. Even colour was matched to its original in nature: the 1952 'Petal' gown (The Metropolitan Museum of Art) combines ivory silk taffeta for the lower skirt with green silk velvet for the bodice and a petal-like formation at the waist. (The first version of 1949 was black velvet and white taffeta.) No Eve or Rima of the wilderness has been more fully arrayed in the elements of the environment than the woman who wears this dress. Yet the shaping is unyielding, with a defiance of body naturalism; this budding flower is, as it were, made of iron. James favoured such colours as shell-like pink and pale waterlily green.

James's sports and children's wear showed the designer's easier side. Though limited in number, his inventive sportswear – sometimes conceived as wonderful separates for his elite clients, or else designed for James's popular licences – depended on simplification. Side-saddle and tulip skirts of the 1950s and sweetly happy children's clothing are characterized by an American liking for comfort in both construction and wearing. Evening dresses of the 1930s and 1950s learned from sportswear, including a 1937 evening dress with halter top constructed from the origami of extended panels from the skirt.

I n the end, however, James will always be remembered for the silent sentinels he created as monumental sculptures in fabric. His 1940s and 1950s work is his most famous and yet it is his most treacherous in terms of design. His proclamations of design probity were regularly betrayed in this work by his need to add more and more interior structure to achieve the majestic effect of the outer structure. Drawings (whether James's own analytical studies or the later evocative drawings of Antonio) make James a modernist, striving for integral form, but the memorable ballgowns of the 1940s and 1950s suggest that he was an historical fantasist, one who longed for court elegance and Second Empire magnificence.

The term 'genius' is often used to describe James and he certainly possessed the explosive temperament often associated with the word. But his achievement is, in truth, less than that of a genius. He compromised his 1930s elegance with his work in the 1940s and 1950s and his pictorial imagination came to surpass his design inno-vation. So he was probably not a genius, but he was surely close enough to being one that we can still look at his dresses with a combi-nation of awe and the more modest respect. T. S. Eliot has said that April mixes 'memory and desire'. In fashion, no one mingles them more persuasively than Charles James.

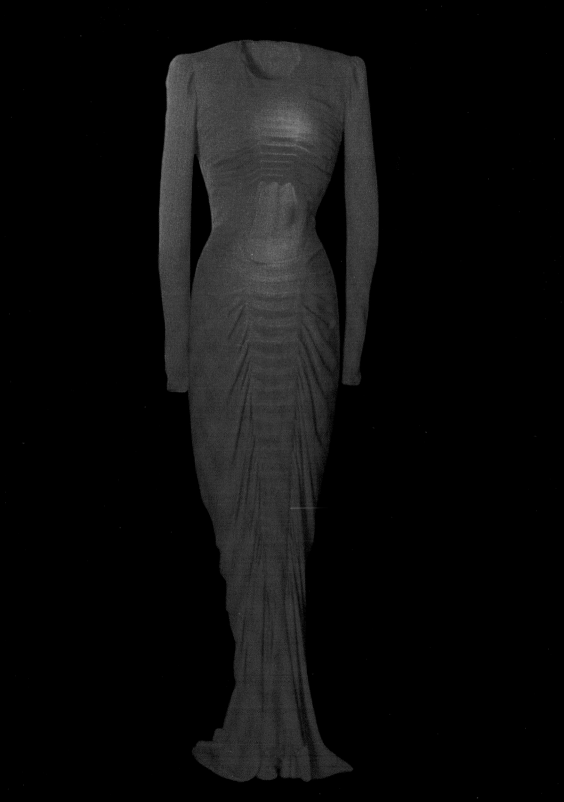

long eve & dinner.

eve coat in white.

black Ja

*White
alencon
& corded*

14 of

6 of - Ankle.

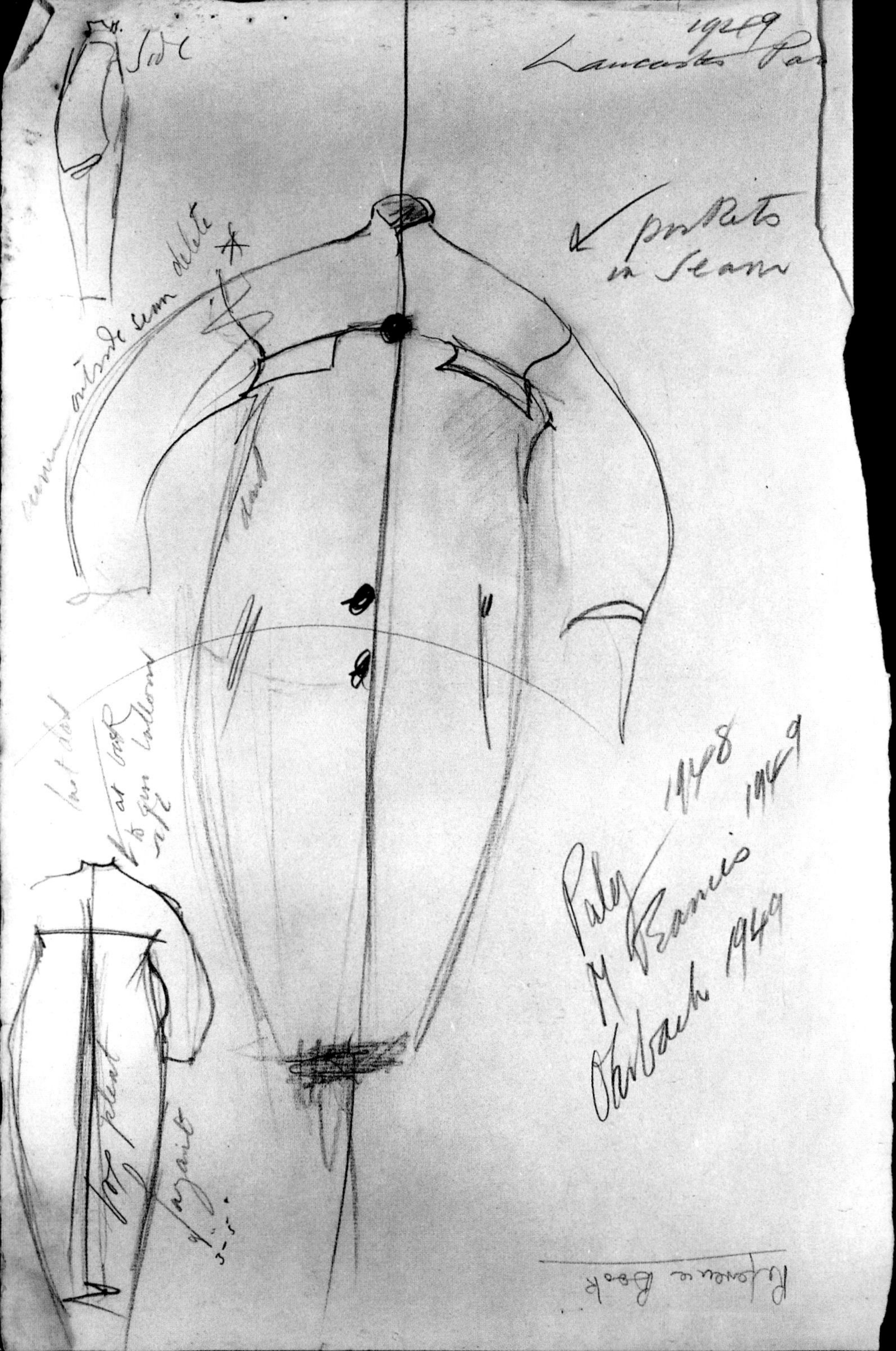

1929

Lancaster Pa

← pocket in seam

Side

Paley 1948
M Francis 1949
Ohrbach 1949

Reference Book

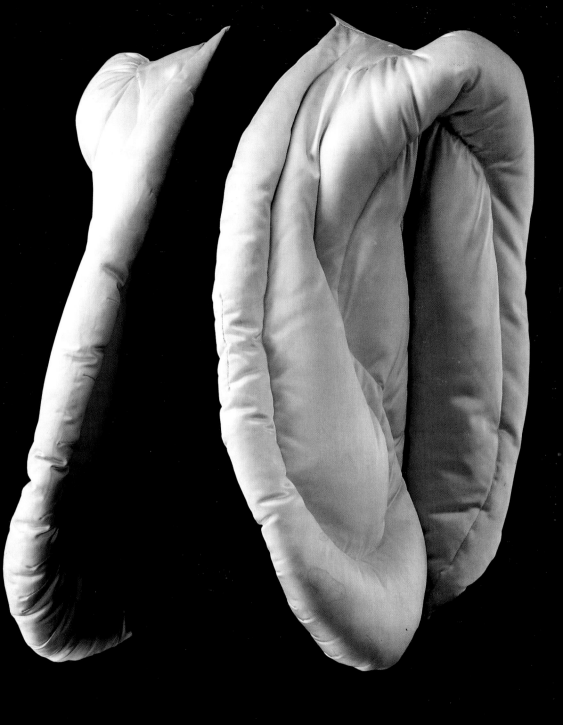

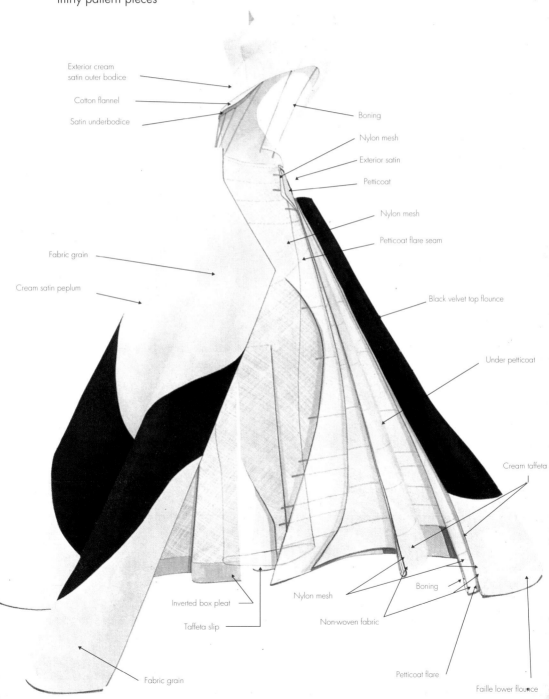

Study for the 'Four-leaf Clover' evening gown. The gown is constructed from thirty pattern pieces

Exterior cream satin outer bodice

Cotton flannel

Satin underbodice

Boning

Nylon mesh

Exterior satin

Petticoat

Nylon mesh

Petticoat flare seam

Fabric grain

Cream satin peplum

Black velvet top flounce

Under petticoat

Cream taffeta

Inverted box pleat

Taffeta slip

Nylon mesh

Non-woven fabric

Boning

Fabric grain

Petticoat flare

Faille lower flounce

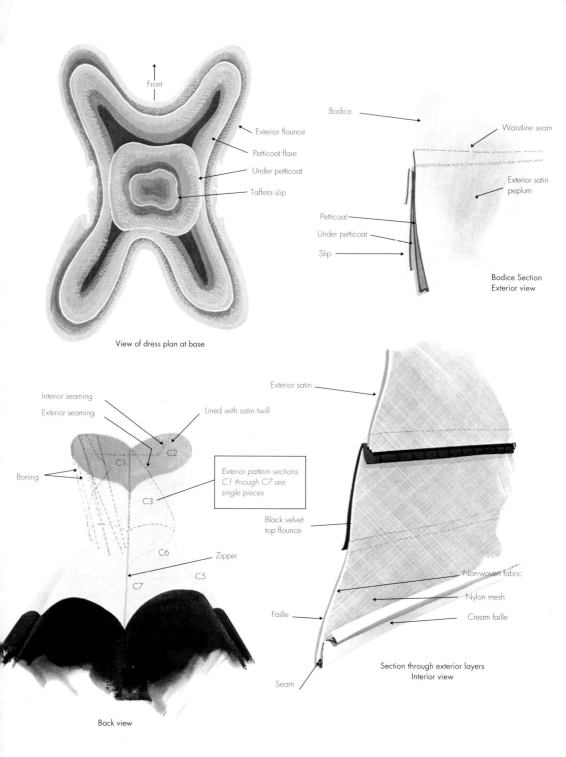

Front

Exterior flounce

Petticoat flare

Under petticoat

Taffeta slip

View of dress plan at base

Bodice

Waistline seam

Exterior satin
peplum

Petticoat

Under petticoat

Slip

Bodice Section
Exterior view

Interior seaming

Exterior seaming

Lined with satin twill

C2

C1

Boning

C3

Exterior pattern sections
C1 through C7 are
single pieces

C6

Zipper

C7

C5

Back view

Exterior satin

Black velvet
top flounce

Non-woven fabric

Nylon mesh

Cream faille

Faille

Seam

Section through exterior layers
Interior view

EVNG WRAP

deep
Brown *velut.*
medium
& faille *short*

wrap.

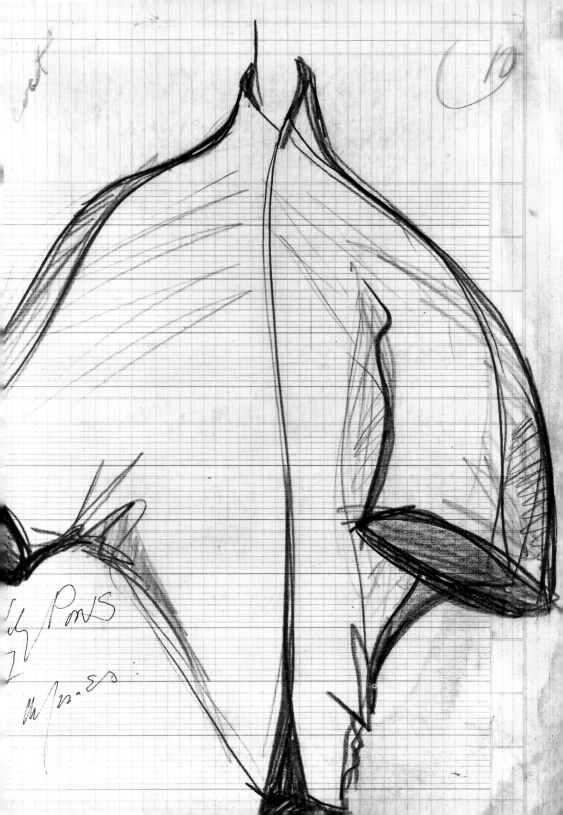

Chronology

1906   Born on 18 July in Sandhurst, England, to an English father and an American mother.

1919– 1922   Attends Harrow School, where he meets Evelyn Waugh, Francis Rose and, most importantly, Cecil Beaton, with whom he forms a longstanding friendship. Expelled from Harrow for a 'sexual escapade'.

1926   At the age of nineteen, Charles James opens his first hat shop in Chicago, using the name of a schoolfriend, 'Charles Boucheron'.

1928   Leaves Chicago for Long Island with 70 cents, a Pierce Arrow and a number of hats as his only possessions. Opens a hat shop above a garage in Murray Hill, New York. Begins his first dress designs.

1930– 1940   Dividing his time between London, Paris and New York, James begins to sell his designs to department stores, including the new Fortnum & Mason's in New York.

1933   Presents a collection of town and country wear which is later marketed by Roberts Dresses.

1934   With financial support from his mother and friends, James presents a collection in the Wedgwood Room of Marshall Field & Co., Chicago. Receives his first commissions for theatre costumes.

1937   Shows his first Paris collection, following which his designs are bought by Harrods in London and Bergdorf Goodman in New York.

1940   Settles in New York.

1943– 1945   Designs for the Elizabeth Arden fashion department.

The arcs in the hem of this apron skirt echo the form of the heart-shaped neckline, producing an effect of sweet innocence, falsely provincial and naive, but also conceived deliberately as a repetition of form.
© Photo: Cecil Beaton, 1948. Courtesy Sotheby's, London.

1945	Elizabeth Arden's new store opens with a benefit evening for the Red Cross; twenty-five of Charles James's creations are shown.
1947	Makes a brief but triumphant return to the world of Parisian haute couture.
1948	The retrospective exhibition 'Decade of Design' opens at the Brooklyn Museum in New York showing dresses created by Charles James for his greatest American patron, Millicent Rogers.
1950	Awarded a 'Winnie', the Coty American Fashion Critics Award, for his 'magical use of colour and artistic mastery of drapery'.
1954	Marries Nancy Lee Gregory, with whom he has two children. Following the birth of Charles James Jr. in 1956, James designs his first collections for children. The marriage breaks up in 1961. James concentrates increasingly on his designs for the mass market.
1958	After numerous business failures, James retreats from the public eye, bankrupt.
1964	Moves into the Chelsea Hotel in New York, where he establishes a small studio but attracts very few clients. He begins to design jewelry, with little success. Meets the illustrator Antonio Lopez, who, over the following years, draws the best of James's designs.
1975	Solo exhibition at the Everson Museum of Art, Syracuse, New York.
1978	Dies alone, of pneumonia, at the Chelsea Hotel, New York.
1980	Large retrospective exhibition at the Brooklyn Museum.

Barbara Paley wearing an evening or ball-gown. This same design was ordered by eight of the couturier's most prestigious clients.
Photo: John Rawlings for Vogue USA.

Charles James

James's modernity and the eroticism of his designs is highlighted by a contemporary photographer. © Bruce Weber.
'Swan' ball-gown. Draped bodice and black chiffon and tulle skirt in the 'draped apron' style. Design created for Jennifer Jones. Photo: Irving Solaro. © The Museum at Fashion Institute of Technology.

The James Encyclopaedia by Beaton. Beaton recognized James's aspiration to epic historicism. The underskirts of James's dresses evoke the brilliance and love of luxury characteristic of the Second Empire, a world entirely inhabited by women of flawless beauty. © Photo: Cecil Beaton, 1948. Courtesy Sotheby's, London.

Artist and model. James's marriage, surprising in a life inclined to homosexuality and implicitly to misogyny, surely centred on the ideal of femininity. We see him observing the new bride, who personifies his ideal of the elegant and feminine woman. He would always remain a passionate observer of domestic, feminine beauty. © Photo: Cecil Beaton, 1955. Courtesy Sotheby's, London.

James's main concern in the 1930s led him to concentrate his work on the front of the dress, creating a symmmetry in the pleating and lines that emanated from the central column, whose suppleness was reminiscent of ancient caryatids. Photo: Irving Solaro. © The Museum at Fashion Institute of Technology.
Evelyn Tripp wearing the short version of the 'Swan' dress. © Photo: Horst P. Horst, 1951.

Artist and studio. An ascetic of stormy and artistic temperament, James is captured here in all his vanity and diversity by a photographer and aesthete influenced by Surrealism. © Photo: Cecil Beaton, 1929. Courtesy Sotheby's, London. **Beaton's view** of James's studio in 1944, just prior to the latter's own representation of the 'New Look', bears witness to the couturier's talent in the handling of drapery. Drawing by Cecil Beaton published in *Vogue USA*. © All rights reserved.

The 'Sirène'. The most celebrated of all James's gowns is an exercise based on the wrapping of pliant materials around a rigid inner structure. The bust and the central part of the dress front are supported by an infrastructure, also draped so as to create the illusion of an unrestricted and fluid form. Photos: Irving Solaro. © The Museum at Fashion Institute of Technology, gift of Doris Duke.

During the final period of James's life, Antonio was one of the couturier's ardent admirers. Here, this superb illustrator offers a synthesis of five of James's celebrated designs. His scrupulous knowledge of the garments enabled him to distinguish each model by a characteristic trait and to restore its full suppleness. Drawing: Antonio Lopez. © The Museum at Fashion Institute of Technology, gift of Juan Ramos.

Drawing by Charles James. © All rights reserved.
High-waisted Gothic sheath dress with bow at bust height, and the same dress with a matching jacket. Photographer unknown. Published in *US Harper's Bazaar*. © All rights reserved.

Seams as decoration. By transforming the necessary seams on his coats into visible lines, James succeeded in embellishing his designs without resorting to anything other than the seam lines themselves. Detail of suit jacket. © Richard Avedon, 1955.
'Egyptian' or 'Pagoda' tunic suit, 1954. Photo: Lillian Bassman, published in *US Harper's Bazaar* in 1955. © All rights reserved.

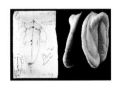

In this 1949 coat the egg-shape would appear to be restricting, but a rear view shows the deep central pleat which allows movement. Sketch by Charles James. Courtesy of The Brooklyn Museum Collection.
In '400 Years of Fashion', the Victoria and Albert Museum described this forerunner of the anorak as a 'cult object of the seventies', when the idea was taken up again by Halston. © Courtesy of the Board of Trustees of the Victoria and Albert Museum.

Drawing by Charles James. The Brooklyn Museum, gift of Mrs William Randolph Hearst.
James often preferred the curves and pleats inspired by the kimono to the rectilinear shapes of certain garments. The collars were either enormous or entirely absent. Here they describe arcs which form an uninterrupted line with those of the capes. Photo: John Rawlings, published in *Vogue USA* in August 1947. © 1947 (renewed 1975) by The Condé Nast Publications, Inc.

Detail and decorum. In these two dresses, the absence of decorative surfaces is tempered by the use of a construction consisting of subtle pleats and visible seams which constitute the only ornament. © Courtesy of the Board of Trustees of the Victoria and Albert Museum. Photo: Erwin Blumenfeld, published in *Vogue USA* in April 1947. © 1947 (renewed 1975) by The Condé Nast Publications, Inc.

Draped on the model. James possessed the rare gift of draping straight onto the model, working directly with the fabric. The couturier's designs were tried out in this way rather than being worked up from drawings and made into patterns. Through his use of draping, James was able to continue the development of body-clinging clothing. Photo published in *Look*, 2 January 1955. © All rights reserved. Drawing: Antonio Lopez. © Galerie Chariau-Bartsch.

A well-defined silhouette was essential in James's eyes. In a ball-gown of 1954, a prominent bust protrudes above a skirt as ample às Dior's scissor dresses. Photo: Irving Solaro. © The Museum at Fashion Institute of Technology. **The 'Tulip' dress** of 1949 allows a burst of fabric to unfurl at the knee. Photo published in *US Harper's Bazaar* in July 1949. © Richard Avedon, 1949.

Form and void. As a rule, James used light and dark to split the mass of the dress into an artful visual enigma, as the dress designed for Lisa Kirk illustrates. Photo: Irving Solaro. © The Museum at Fashion Institute of Technology, gift of Robert Wells.
Mrs Hearst, wearing a variation on the 'Four-leaf Clover' ball-gown, in white taffeta and pink satin. Photo published in *Look* in 1953. © All rights reserved.

The return of splendour. James's ball-gowns of the late forties and the fifties revealed his penchant for the splendour of the historical style, worthy of the House of Worth (creators of English haute couture in Paris). 'Four-leaf Clover' ball-gown in taffeta and satin. Photos: Irving Solaro. © The Museum at Fashion Institute of Technology.

James's 'Four-leaf Clover' evening dress (1953). © Courtesy of the Board of Trustees of the Victoria and Albert Museum. This dress demonstrates **James's skill** in contrasting a stiff interior with a supple exterior. Once the interior framework had been created, a fluid surface was applied – reflected here in the treatment of the back of the bodice. Drawing by Bill Wilkinson, 1982. © All rights reserved.

This dress conveys the impression of fluttering movement despite the sewing together of built-up, superimposed layers radiating from a central core with its most slender point at the waist. Drawing by Bill Wilkinson, 1982. © All rights reserved.
In the celebrated 'Petal' ball-gown, the tight bodice and the yoke at the hips are adopted in contrast to the flowering of the skirt. © Horst P. Horst, 1951.

Dress created in 1955 with a skirt covered in six layers of tulle. Photo: Irving Solaro. © The Museum at Fashion Institute of Technology.
The same dress with pleated effect in taffeta as portrayed by Bruce Weber. © Photo: Bruce Weber.

Sketch by Charles James for the 'Balloon' dress.
© The Brooklyn Museum Collection.
Creativity and circumference. In a photograph taken in 1952, James appears as a successful designer, arranging hoops similar to those of a crinoline around a dressmaker's dummy, itself an archetype of the society woman. Photo published in *Look* in 1952. © All rights reserved.

The 'Balloon' dress. With this dress of 1955, James created a brilliant pastiche of historical styles: high Empire waistline, a full skirt recalling the wide circumferences of the Second Empire, bare shoulders reminiscent of the paintings of Ingres and accentuated pouf dress characteristic of the late eighteenth century. Despite this, James produced a dress that was modern with clean-cut lines. Drawing by Antonio Lopez. © Galerie Chariau-Bartsch. Photo: Unknown photographer. © All rights reserved.

This evening outfit of 1950 illustrates James's concern with décolletage. His structured bodices permitted the rigid form to embrace this bold neckline at the front. Photo: Fonssagrives, published in *Town and Country*. © Fonssagrives, 1949.
Arcs and pleats come into play in the turned-down sleeves of this dress and in the cubism of the little cape, with the abrupt emergence of an angular neckline. Photo: de Faurer, published in *Flair*. © All rights reserved.

Exploration of form. Drawing by Charles James. © All rights reserved.
Concern for line in this smart, feminine outfit, perfectly finished but nevertheless relaxed, thanks to the detail on the sleeves. Photo: Erwin Blumenfeld. Courtesy *Vogue USA.* © 1947 (renewed 1975) by The Condé Nast Publications, Inc.

Long before the fashion for one-size-fits-all, Balenciaga, like James, created roomy dresses and cocoon-shaped silhouettes. These ample kimonos were extremely comfortable since they lacked buttons or any other type of fastening. Photo: Horst, published in *Vogue USA* in February 1950. © Horst P. Horst, 1950.
James's preparatory drawing for the coat designed for Lily Pons in 1947. Courtesy of The Brooklyn Museum.

Apparitions in evening capes. In a photograph by Cecil Beaton (1936), four evening cloaks by James act as silent sentinels who are aware of their sculptural potential, but who are likewise transformed into spectres rather than real women. Photo: Cecil Beaton, published in *Vogue USA* in November 1936. © 1936 (renewed 1964) by The Condé Nast Publications, Inc.

Although Cinderella was James's final fantasy in the style of his ball-gowns, this Goya-like combination of mysterious, ecclesiastic and crepuscular dignity represented James's ideal for evening capes. Photo: Cecil Beaton, published in *Vogue USA* in November 1936. © 1936 (renewed 1964) by The Condé Nast Publications, Inc.

Captions translated from the French by Ruth Taylor

The publishers wish to thank Bruce Weber, Richard Avedon, Horst P. Horst, Lillian Bassman, John Rawlings, Fernand Fonssagrives, Irving Solaro and François Baudot.
    This book could not have been produced without the invaluable assistance of Dorothy Twining Globus (The Museum at Fashion Institute of Technology), Tiggy Manonochie (Hamilton Photographers), Erika Sipos (Little Bear), Lorraine Mead (The Condé Nast Publications), David (*Harper's Bazaar*), Lydia Cresswell-Jones (Sotheby's, London) and Brian Hetherington (Richard Avedon Studio).
    Our thanks to them all.